D0254206

ACKNOWLEDGEMENTS

Publishing Director	Piers Pickard
Commissioning Editor	Catharine Robertson
Assistant Editor	Christina Webb
Illustrators	Andy Mansfield
	Sebastien Iwohn
Designer	Andy Mansfield
Print production	Larissa Frost,
	Nigel Longuet
With thanks to	Rei Uemura,
	Laura Crawford

Published in March 2018 by Lonely Planet Global Ltd
CRN: 554153
ISBN: 978 1 78701 270 7
www.lonelyplanetkids.com
© Lonely Planet 2018
Printed in China

10 9 8 7 6 5 4 3 2

Lonely Planet Offices

AUSTRALIA
The Malt Store, Level 3, 551 Swanston St,
Carlton, Victoria 3053
T: 03 8379 8000

IRELAND
Digital Depot, Roe Lane (off Thomas St), Digital Hub,
Dublin 8, D08 TCV4

USA
124 Linden St, Oakland, CA 94607
T: 510 250 6400

UK
240 Blackfriars Rd, London SE1 8NW
T: 020 3771 5100

STAY IN TOUCH lonelyplanet.com/contact

first words
JAPANESE

Illustrated by
Andy Mansfield & Sebastien Iwohn

hello

こんにちは

konnichiwa

(kon-ni-chi-wa)

ice cream

アイスクリーム
aisukuriimu
(ais-ku-ree-mu)

water
みず
mizu
(mi-zu)

supermarket

スーパーマーケット

sūpāmāketto

(soo-pah-mah-ket-to)

shopping cart

ショッピングカート
shoppingu kāto
(shop-pin-gu kah-to)

cat

ねこ

neko

(ne-ko)

bus

バス
basu
(ba-su)

dress

ワンピース

wanpiisu

(wan-pee-su)

dog

いぬ
inu
(i-nu)

banana

バナナ

banana

(ba-na-na)

duck

かも

kamo

(ka-mo)

taxi
___
タクシー
takushii
(tak-shee)

t-shirt

ティーシャツ
tiishatsu
(tee-sha-tsu)

fish

さかな
sakana
(sa-ka-na)

airplane

ひこうき
hikōki
(hi-koh-ki)

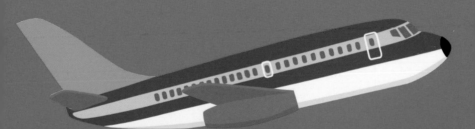

chopsticks
はし
hashi
(ha-shi)

noodles

ラーメン

rāmen

(rah-men)

swimming pool

プール

pūru

(poo-ru)

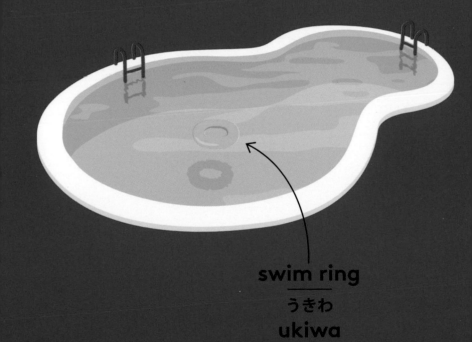

swim ring

うきわ

ukiwa

(u-ki-wa)

cheese

チーズ
chiizu
(chee-zu)

bowl

ボウル
bōru

(boh-ru)

doctor

おいしゃさん

oishasan

(oy-sha-san)

apple

りんご

ringo

(rin-go)

worm
—
むし
mushi
(mu-shi)

beach

ビーチ

biichi

(bee-chi)

bicycle

じてんしゃ
jitensha
(ji-ten-sha)

airport

くうこう

kūkō

(koo-koh)

juice

ジュース

jūsu

(joo-su)

market

いちば

ichiba

(i-chi-ba)

shoes

くつ

kutsu

(ku-tsu)

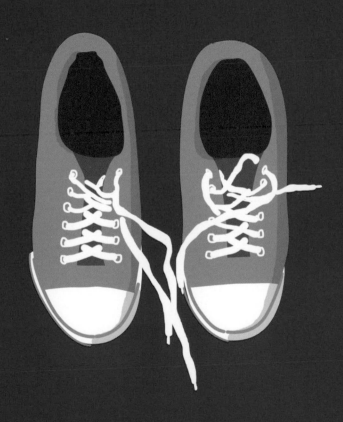

phone

でんわ

denwa

(den-wa)

post office

ゆうびんきょく

yūbinkyoku

(yoo-bin-kyo-ku)

restaurant

レストラン

resutoran

(res-to-ran)

hotel

ホテル

hoteru

(ho-te-ru)

milk

ぎゅうにゅう

gyūnyū

(gyoo-nyoo)

chocolate

チョコレート

chokorēto

(cho-ko-ray-to)

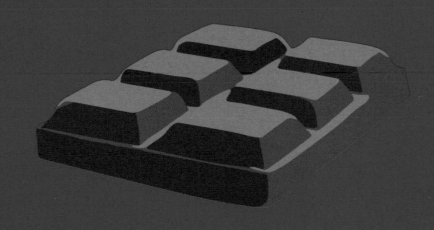

car

くるま

kuruma

(ku-ru-ma)

hat

ぼうし
bōshi
(boh-shi)

sunglasses

サングラス

sangurasu
(san-gu-ra-su)

chicken

チキン
chikin

(chi-kin)

train

でんしゃ
densha
(den-sha)

station

えき

eki

(e-ki)

clock
とけい
tokei
(to-kay)

toilet

トイレ

toire

(toy-re)

bed

ベッド
beddo
(bed-do)

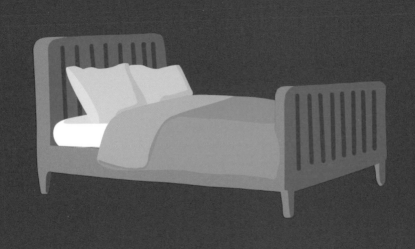

house

いえ
ie
(ih-eh)

chimney

えんとつ
entotsu
(en-to-tsu)

pants

ズボン

zubon

(zu-bon)

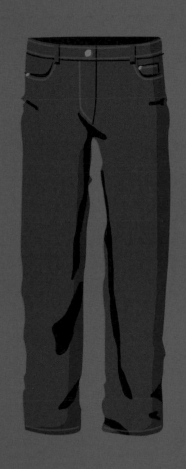

suitcase

スーツケース

sūtsukēsu

(soots-kay-su)

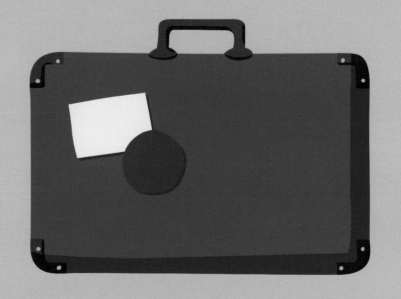

plate

さら

sara

(sa-ra)

knife

ナイフ
naifu
(nai-fu)

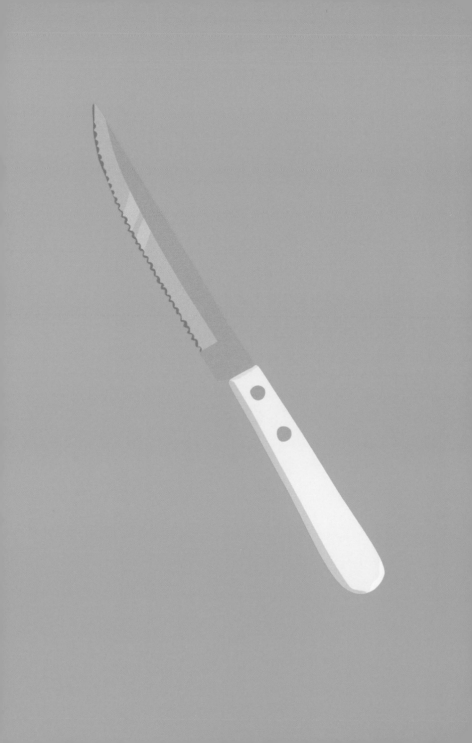

fork

フォーク
fōku
(foh-ku)

spoon

スプーン

supūn

(s-poon)

computer

コンピューター

konpyūtā

(kon-pyoo-tah)

mouse

マウス

mausu

(mau-su)

book

ほん

hon

(hon)

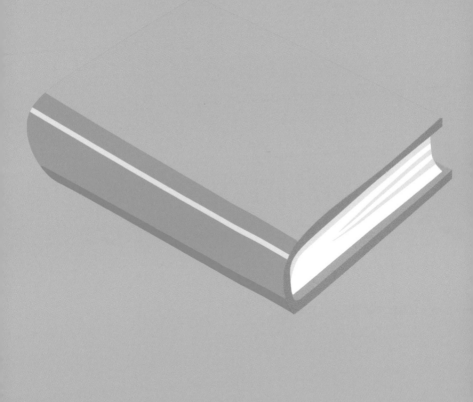

sandwich

サンドイッチ
sandoitchi
(san-doh-it-chi)

yes
はい
hai
(hai)

no
いいえ
iie
(ee-eh)

movie theater

えいがかん

eigakan

(ay-ga-kan)

park

こうえん

kōen

(koh-en)

menu

メニュー

menyū
(men-yoo)

passport

パスポート

pasupōto

(pas-paw-toh)

police officer

おまわりさん

omawarisan

(o-ma-wa-ri-san)

key

かぎ

kagi
(ka-gi)

ticket

きっぷ
kippu
(kip-pu)

sushi

すし

sushi

(su-shi)

rain

あめ

ame

(a-meh)

snow

—

ゆき

yuki

(yu-ki)

sun

———

たいよう

taiyō

(tai-yoh)

tree

き

ki

(ki)

flower

はな

hana

(ha-na)

cake

ケーキ
kēki
(kay-ki)

cherry

さくらんぼ
sakuranbo
(sa-ku-ram-bo)

ball

ボール
bō-ru
(boh-ru)

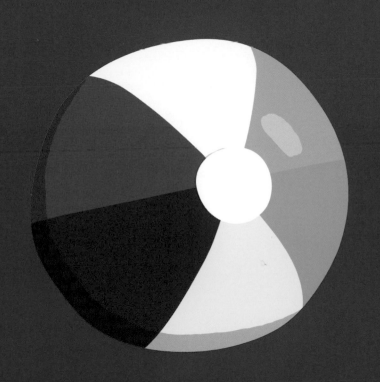

bird

とり

tori

(to-ri)

egg

たまご

tamago

(ta-ma-go)

umbrella

かさ

kasa

(ka-sa)

panda

パンダ

panda

(pan-da)

money

おかね

okane

(o-ka-ne)

bank

ぎんこう
ginkō
(gin-koh)

mouse

ねずみ

nezumi

(ne-zu-mi)

scarf

マフラー
mafurā
(ma-fu-rah)

gloves

てぶくろ

tebukuro

(te-bu-ku-ro)

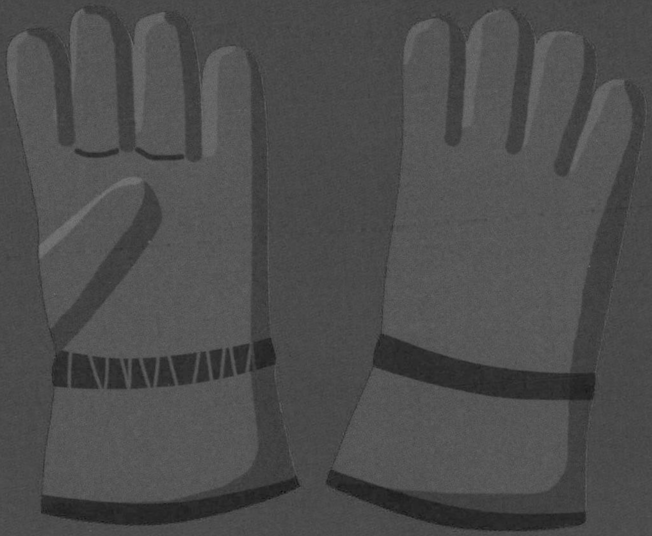

coat

コート

kōto

(koh-to)

hospital

びょういん

byōin

(byoh-in)

chair

いす
isu
(i-su)

table

テーブル

tēburu

(tay-bu-ru)

toothbrush

はブラシ

haburashi

(ha-bu-ra-shi)

toothpaste

はみがきこ

hamigakiko

(ha-mi-ga-ki-ko)

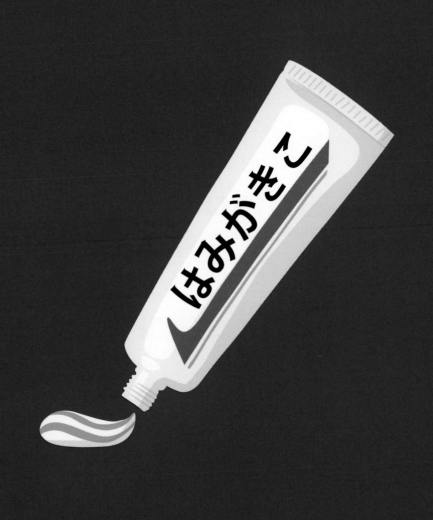

sunscreen

ひやけどめ

hiyakedome

(hi-ya-ke-do-me)

lion

ライオン

raion

(rai-on)

mountain

———

やま

yama

(ya-ma)

monkey
さる
saru
(sa-ru)

spider

くも

kumo

(ku-mo)

rice

ごはん

gohan

(go-han)

pen

ペン

pen

(pen)

door
___
ドア
doa
(do-a)

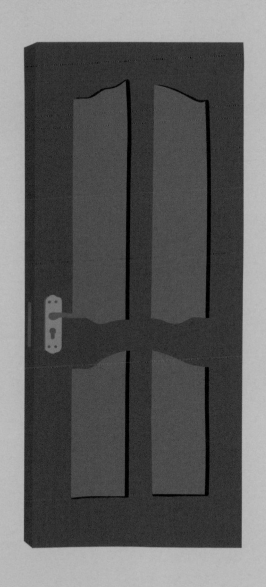

window

まど

mado

(ma-do)

curtain
カーテン
kāten
(kah-ten)

tent

テント

tento

(ten-to)

map

ちず

chizu

(chi-zu)

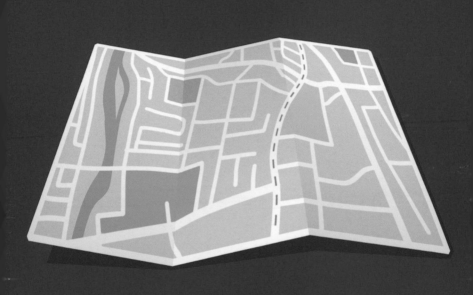

tomato

トマト

tomato

(to-ma-to)

moon

つき

tsuki

(ts-ki)

stars

ほし

hoshi
(ho-shi)

postcard

はがき

hagaki

(ha-ga-ki)

stamp

きって

kitte

(kit-te)

boat

ふね

fune

(fu-ne)

goodbye

さようなら

sayōnara

(sa-yoh-na-ra)